SAM
HOUSTON
TEXAS HERO

William R. Sanford &
Carl R. Green

Enslow Publishers, Inc.

40 Industrial Road   PO Box 38
Box 398   Aldershot
Berkeley Heights, NJ 07922   Hants GU12 6BP
USA   UK

http://www.enslow.com

Library of Congress Cataloging-in-Publication Data

Sanford, William R. (William Reynolds), 1927–
    Sam Houston : Texas Hero / William R. Sanford and Carl R. Green.
        p. cm. — (Legendary heroes of the Wild West)
    Includes bibliographical references and index.
    ISBN 0-89490-651-8
    1. Houston, Sam, 1793–1863—Juvenile literature. 2. Governors —
Texas—Biography—Juvenile literature. 3. Legislators—United States—
Biography—Juvenile literature. 4. United States. Congress. Senate—Biography—
Juvenile literature. I. Green, Carl R. II. Title. III. Series: Sanford, William R.
(William Reynolds), 1927– Legendary heroes of the Wild West.
F390.H84S36 1996
976.4'05'092—dc20
[B]   95-32160
                                         CIP
                                         AC

Printed in the United States of America

10 9 8 7 6 5 4 3

Illustration Credits: Archives Division, Texas State Library, pp. 12, 15, 16,
20, 24; Carl R. Green and William R. Sanford, pp. 8, 28; Texas Department
of Transportation, pp. 6, 9, 31, 33, 36, 39, 40.

Cover Illustration: Paul Daly

CONTENTS

AUTHORS' NOTE

This book tells the true story of Sam Houston. Sam was one of the Old West's greatest heroes. In his day, he was known as an outstanding general and statesman. His daring exploits and fiery speeches were featured in newspapers, magazines, and dime novels. In more recent years, Sam has been the subject of novels, films, and biographies. You may find it hard to believe that one man could pack so much adventure and achievement into a single lifetime. If so, rest easy. All of the events described in this book really happened.

1

THE BATTLE OF
SAN JACINTO

Weary Texans grumbled as they set up camp on the plain of San Jacinto. The date was April 21, 1836. The soldiers were tired of retreating. The Mexican army was camped almost within rifle shot. Would General Sam Houston ever let them stand and fight?

A battle had been brewing for weeks. Leading the Mexicans was General Antonio López de Santa Anna. The Mexican dictator was trying to crush the Texans' fight for independence. He had begun by marching on San Antonio. On March 6, his troops had stormed the Alamo. All of the defenders had died in that bloody battle. At Goliad, he had ordered the slaughter of almost four hundred prisoners. Now only Sam Houston and his tiny army were left to defend Texas.

Tall oak trees trailed a curtain of Spanish moss over the Texans' camp. Less than a mile away, Santa Anna's men built a barricade of brush and baggage. The dictator felt certain the outnumbered Texans would not attack. The barricade finished, his men stacked their rifles and fell asleep.

Santa Anna's confidence seemed well founded. He commanded 1,250 men to Sam Houston's 910.[1] Sam's best hope lay in the deadeye shooting of his riflemen. He waited, hoping the Mexicans would attack.

The hours dragged past. All at once, Sam took a bold step. He sent the famous scout Deaf Smith riding west to

On April 21, 1836, two armies faced each other at San Jacinto, near Galveston Bay. The Texans were led by General Sam Houston. The Mexican forces fought under Antonio López de Santa Anna. Houston led the charge that broke the Mexican lines and insured Texas independence.

burn Vince's Bridge. With the bridge down, Santa Anna's reinforcements could not reach him. Water and marshy ground made retreat difficult. This would be a fight to the finish.

At 3:30 P.M., Sam was ready. He mounted his white horse and led his men forward. The advancing soldiers flanked two small cannon called the Twin Sisters. Houston rode up and down the line. "Hold your fire, men. Hold your fire," he urged.[2] His silent troops pressed forward through the tall grass. A reserve force waited in the cover of the trees.

When the sleeping enemy lay only two hundred yards away, Sam waved his hat. The Twin Sisters roared. With grapeshot in short supply, the gunners had loaded the cannon with scrap metal. Chunks of broken horseshoes ripped through the barricade. The Texans surged forward. As they ran, they yelled, "Remember the Alamo!"[3]

Santa Anna's men groped for their guns. A few wild shots peppered the attacking Texans. Sam's white horse went down. Sam jumped free, grabbed a second horse, and swung into the saddle. A moment later a musket ball shattered his ankle. The second horse fell under him. Somehow, Sam pulled himself onto a third horse.

The Texans broke through what was left of the barricade. Many of the Mexicans fought bravely. Others ran for their lives. Santa Anna, unnerved by the assault, fled on horseback. Eighteen minutes after the first shots were fired, the battle was over.

"¡Me no Alamo!" frightened Mexicans pleaded.[4] The

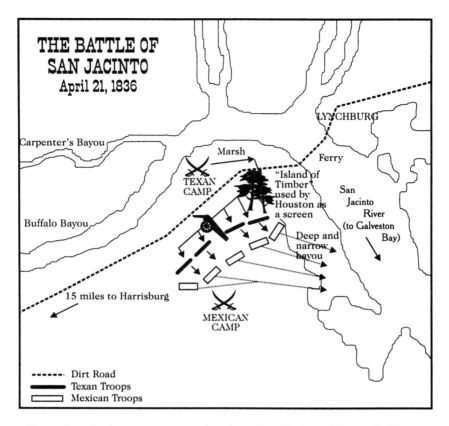

THE BATTLE OF
SAN JACINTO
April 21, 1836

LYNCHBURG

Carpenter's Bayou

Marsh

Ferry

TEXAN
CAMP

"Island of
Timber"
used by
Houston as
a screen

San
Jacinto
River
(to Galveston
Bay)

Buffalo Bayou

Deep and
narrow
bayou

15 miles to Harrisburg

MEXICAN
CAMP

----- Dirt Road
▬▬▬ Texan Troops
▢ Mexican Troops

Even though they were outnumbered at San Jacinto, Houston's Texans possessed the element of surprise. They fought like demons, inspired by their battle cries of "Remember the Alamo! Remember Goliad." The Mexican forces broke and ran after putting up a brief resistance.

Texans were beyond caring. Blind with rage, they shot, clubbed, and knifed hundreds of helpless men. When the dust settled, six hundred thirty Mexicans lay dead. Another six hundred thirty had surrendered. More than two hundred of them had been wounded. Only two Texans had been killed in the surprise attack, although seven more died later of their wounds.[5]

A patrol found Santa Anna the next day. The riders brought the dictator back to camp. They found Sam sitting under a tree, nursing his wounded ankle. Santa Anna feared he would be sent to a firing squad. Sam had a better idea. He offered to spare the dictator's life—if all Mexican troops left Texas. Santa Anna quickly wrote the orders that sent his men home.

The stroke of Santa Anna's pen ended the Texas war for independence. Thanks to Sam Houston and his brave soldiers, Texas was free.

When revenge-minded Texans captured Santa Anna, many of them wanted to hang the Mexican leader. Sam Houston, still suffering the pain of a bullet wound in the ankle, had a better idea. The canny general offered to spare Santa Anna's life in return for Texan independence.

2

GROWING UP IN A NEW COUNTRY

~~~~~~~~~~~~

In 1793 the United States was still a very young country. Most of its four million people lived near the Atlantic coast. The great surge westward was still to come.

On March 2, Elizabeth Houston of Timber Ridge plantation gave birth to her fifth son. She named the boy Sam. The name was a tribute to her husband, Major Samuel Houston. Two days later President George Washington began his second term.

Timber Ridge lay in a sunny valley near Lexington, Virginia. Slaves worked in the fields and helped out in the big house. Major Houston, an inspector in the state militia, was seldom home. While he was gone, Elizabeth managed the plantation. She had little time to care for an infant. A slave girl took care of Sam.[1]

Four more babies arrived over the next few years. Left free to wander the nearby woods, Sam learned to hunt, fish, and swim. When he was eight, Elizabeth sent him to a log schoolhouse. Although he often cut class, Sam mastered reading and writing. At home, his father filled his head with stories of the young nation's heroes. In his free time, Sam read books on geography and history.

Major Houston paid his travel costs out of his own pocket. In time his debts outstripped his income. The Houstons talked of selling out and moving west. The major's sudden death in 1807 made the move even more urgent.[2]

Elizabeth sold Timber Ridge and bought land in eastern Tennessee. The family piled its belongings into two wagons and headed west. The three hundred mile journey to the new farm near Maryville took three weeks. This was truly the frontier. The Cherokee Nation owned the land on the far side of the nearby river.

Sam's older brothers carved a farm from the wilderness. Sam did his share, but he was bored by farming. For a time, he went back to school. There he fell in love with Homer's epic work, *The Iliad*. Sam never forgot those stirring tales. Like Homer's ancient Greek heroes, he believed he was destined for greatness.[3]

As the farm prospered, Sam's brothers invested in a dry goods store. After Sam quit school at sixteen, they put him to work as a clerk. Sam hated this job, too. When he felt too tied down, he vanished into the woods. One day he did not return.

Weeks later, the Houstons heard that Sam was living with the Cherokees. Two of his older brothers set out to bring him home. When they reached the Indian village, they found Sam reading a book. The teenager refused to go home with them. He said he "preferred measuring deer tracks to [measuring] tape."[4]

In time, Chief John Jolly adopted Sam. Sam, in turn, learned the tribe's language and customs. With the other

From the age of sixteen on, Sam Houston was a friend of the Cherokee. Wearing a Cherokee headress, he sat for this painting in Washington, D.C., in 1830.

young men, he played the rough ball game that later became lacrosse. He also took pride in his Cherokee name, *Co-lon-neh* (the Raven).[5] In tribal lore, the raven was both bold and wise. To repay the Cherokees, Sam gave them powder and shot that he bought on credit.

In 1812 Sam took a job as a teacher to pay off his debts. Young Houston, the Maryville townsfolk sneered, had gone to the "Indian university." The jeers did not bother Sam. He was weak in math, but he knew history and geography. More to the point, he was an inspiring teacher. The price to study with Sam was high—eight dollars a term. Parents paid one-third in cash, one-third in corn, and one-third in cloth.

Years later, Sam talked about his teaching days. He said he felt at that time "a higher . . . self-satisfaction than from any office or honor which I have since held."[6] Those good feelings lasted only six months. With his debts paid, Sam went looking for a more heroic career.

3

THE HERO OF
HORSESHOE BEND

～～～～～～～～～～～～～

The War of 1812 changed Sam Houston's life forever. Once again the former colonies found themselves at war with Great Britain. At sea, British warships forced American sailors to join the British navy. On land, British agents stirred up trouble with the Native Americans.

Recruiters for the U.S. Army reached Maryville in March 1813. At the courthouse, an officer put a pile of silver dollars on a drumhead. Sam was one of the men who stepped forward to pick up one of the coins. With that act, the volunteers became army privates.[1]

Twenty-year-old Sam could not enlist without his mother's consent. Elizabeth gladly gave her blessing. She also warned him, ". . . while the door of my cottage is open to brave men, it is eternally shut against cowards."[2]

The army needed men like Sam. At 6 feet 3 inches and 240 pounds, he towered over his fellow soldiers. Better still, this auburn-haired giant was one of the few recruits who could read and write. Within a month, Sam had risen from private to sergeant. Three months later he won appointment as an ensign with the 39th Infantry.

In Alabama a band of Creeks went on the warpath. The warriors, who carried bright red war clubs, were known as Red Sticks. On August 13, they attacked Fort Mims. Nearly five hundred settlers died in the massacre that followed.

General Andrew Jackson of Tennessee called out the militia to meet the threat. He soon found that his ill-trained troops lacked discipline. A call went out for army soldiers to help whip his men into shape. In February 1814, the three hundred and sixty regulars of the 39th joined Jackson's command. Ensign Sam Houston led one of the unit's platoons.

Jackson caught up with the Creeks in east-central Alabama. The Red Sticks were dug in at Horseshoe Bend on the Tallapoosa River. A double-walled barricade known as a breastworks

Twenty-year-old Sam Houston enlisted in the army in 1813. As a member of the 39th Infantry, Ensign Sam Houston served as a platoon commander under Andrew Jackson during the War of 1812.

guarded the three hundred-acre neck of land. Muskets poked through loopholes cut into the thick walls. On March 27, Jackson's cannon opened fire on the breastworks. The stout logs held firm.

As he pondered his next move, Jackson saw black smoke rising near the river. A band of loyal Cherokees had crossed the river in canoes. Now they were torching the Creek village. Sensing that the Red Sticks were confused, Jackson ordered an assault.

The men of the 39th led the way. Major L. P. Montgomery reached the top of the wall before he was killed by a musket ball. Waving his sword, Sam led a wave of soldiers over the wall. A moment later he went down with an arrow in his thigh.

As the fighting raged on, Sam ordered a soldier to pull out the arrow. The man tugged, but the barbed point was caught deep in the muscle. "Try again," Sam ordered. "If you fail this time, I will smite you to the earth." The man could see that Sam meant what he said. He yanked hard at the arrow. It came out in a gush of blood and torn flesh. Sam pressed a rag to the wound and hobbled off to find a doctor.[3]

By 4:00 P.M., the last Red Sticks were holed up in a ravine. Jackson called for volunteers to storm their position. Sam picked up a musket and limped forward. A handful of men followed him. They were within five yards of the breastworks when two musket balls smashed Sam's right shoulder. His men carried him back to safety.

Jackson tried a new tactic. At his orders, a barrage of fire arrows set the Red Stick fort aflame. Marksmen cut down the last warriors as they fled. The Battle of Horseshoe Bend was over.

A surgeon worked on Sam's shoulder. He quit with the job half done, certain Sam would die. To his surprise, his patient survived that pain-filled night. By morning Sam had regained a little strength. Two months later, a horse litter carried him to his mother's house. At first, Elizabeth did not know him. Only the look in Sam's eyes told her this pale, gaunt figure was her son.[4]

4

A WAR HERO
TURNS POLITICIAN

Sam came home a hero, but the price was high. His wounds troubled him the rest of his life. By October 1814, he felt strong enough to visit Washington, D.C. There the newly commissioned lieutenant saw the damage caused by the British raid in August. "My blood boiled" at the sight of the burned buildings, Sam said later.[1]

When the war ended in 1815, Sam stayed in the army. Sent to New Orleans, the tall lieutenant with the grey-blue eyes was a welcome guest at parties. If Sam had a fault, it lay in his taste for whiskey. In fun-loving New Orleans, he had plenty of company.

By 1817 settlers were pushing onto Cherokee land. Sam was assigned the job of persuading his Cherokee friends to move to Arkansas. When the tribe's leaders traveled to Washington for talks, Sam went with them. The Cherokee wore their splendid robes to a reception given by President Monroe. Secretary of War John C. Calhoun was outraged when Sam showed up in his own tribal outfit. Because Sam took their side, Chief Jolly's people listened to the Raven. They gave up their land and took the long trail west.[2]

Sam was left with a bad feeling. Was sending his friends to Arkansas the right thing to do? In March 1818, he resigned from the army. Back in Nashville, Sam went to see Andrew Jackson and his wife. Before long the childless Jacksons were treating Sam like a son.

With Jackson as his mentor, Sam chose the law as a career. At that time, law students studied with older lawyers. Judge James Trimble served as Sam's teacher. He told Sam to set aside a year or more to complete his studies. The judge had not counted on his pupil's fine mind. Six months later, Sam breezed through his bar exam. His high marks gave him the right to practice law in Tennessee.

The new lawyer set up practice in the nearby town of Lebanon. In court, his deep voice and quick wit helped him win tough cases. The county's voters picked him to be district attorney. Sam also joined the militia, where he rose quickly in rank. In the fall of 1821, Major General Houston took command of the Tennessee state militia.

Sam took a second big step in 1823. Running unopposed, he won a seat in Congress. There he served with Henry Clay and Daniel Webster. To help the folks back home, he voted to build roads and canals.

Jackson made his first run for president in 1824. He

came in first, but did not win a majority in the electoral college. Lacking a clear winner, the election was thrown into the House of Representatives. Sam tried to swing Clay's support to Jackson, but failed. Clay, who disliked Jackson, helped put John Quincy Adams in the White House. Adams, in turn, chose Clay as secretary of state. Sam was outraged. He charged the two men with making a secret deal.

Clay and the Jackson camp next locked horns over the choice of a postmaster for Nashville. Clay wanted his son-in-law, John Erwin, to have the job. Sam, still angry, wrote a scorching note to President Adams. The note accused postmaster-elect Erwin of having poor morals. To avenge the insult, Erwin's friend William White challenged Sam to a duel. Sam did not back down. Given his choice of weapons, he chose pistols at fifteen paces.[3]

On September 21, the two men met in a pasture. White shot first—and missed. Sam's shot hit

Painted in 1826, this is the earliest known portrait of Sam Houston. At the time, Julia Ann Conner wrote, "The young Congressman was the most popular man in Tennessee." A year later, Sam entered and won the race for governor.

White in the groin. Later, Sam said, "Thank God [White] was injured no worse."[4]

Sam did not let the close call bother him. In 1827 he ran for governor of Tennessee. He campaigned in shiny black trousers, red sash, hunting shirt, and a beaver hat. His platform called for state support of roads and canals, schools, and trade. In a frontier state, it was a good blueprint for growth.

Sam won a two-year term as governor. A year later the people of the United States gave Andrew Jackson his long-sought victory. Governor Houston shared the triumph with the new president. Sam, it was whispered, might one day follow Jackson to the White House.

5

TWO MARRIAGES

~~~~~~~~~~~~~~~~~~~~

Sam tried hard to be a good governor. Even so, he made enemies. Some people disliked him for treating Native Americans fairly. Others hated him for his ties to Andrew Jackson. All agreed that the thirty-five-year-old bachelor drank too much.

Friends advised Sam to marry and settle down. Sam did not argue the point. He had already picked out his bride-to-be. His choice was blond Eliza Allen. A friend described her as "not pretty, but . . . graceful, and queenly."[1]

Eliza was in no rush to marry. Her parents, though, sided with Sam. The Allens wanted to have a governor in the family. Late in December 1828, Eliza said yes. The wedding took place a month later. Robert Allen led his twenty-year-old daughter down a wide staircase. The groom looked splendid in a cloak lined with scarlet satin.

After a short honeymoon, the newlyweds moved into the Nashville Inn.

The marriage was a stormy one. Eliza hated politics. The rough talk and heavy drinking upset her. The strains increased when Sam announced he would seek a second term. In April he found Eliza crying over old love letters.[2] A few harsh words led to too many more. Eliza charged Sam with insane jealousy. Sam said she had never been a loving wife. That may have been true. The sight of his raw, poorly healed wounds may have sickened her.[3]

The outburst settled nothing. Sam left town for a debate. When he returned, he found that Eliza had left him. Sam followed her to the Allen home. The Allens would not let him see Eliza alone. An old aunt kept watch when the two met. Sam knelt and begged Eliza to return. She refused.

Rumors spread that Sam had treated Eliza badly. Angry men burned a dummy dressed to look like the governor. Troops had to be called out to break up the mob. Sam brooded in silence for five days. Then he resigned his office. His enemies laughed, "Poor Houston, rose like a rocket and fell like a stick."[4]

A steamboat carried Sam westward. He drank too much and thought of suicide. In that dark moment, an omen lifted his spirits. As Sam stood on deck one evening, he saw an eagle fly past. The great bird swooped low. Then it flew into the sunset. In that moment, Sam wrote, "I knew that a great destiny waited for me in the West."[5]

Chief Jolly welcomed his adopted son to the tribe's

Houston admired the Roman general Caius Marius (c. 155 B.C.-86 B.C.) The general had also been in exile and made a comeback. In 1831, Houston had his portrait painted as Marius standing among ruins.

Arkansas home. Sam took off his city clothes and put on Cherokee dress. Before long he had taken on the role of peacemaker. Thanks to his efforts, the Cherokees, Osages, and Creeks agreed to live in peace. In October 1829, the Cherokees made him a citizen of their nation. Sam knew it was a great honor.

The Raven set up a trading post on the Arkansas River. Still depressed, he tried to drown his troubles in whiskey. Before long the Cherokees gave him a new name—Big Drunk. In the midst of his sorrows, Sam found love again. He married Chief Jolly's niece, Tiana Rogers. Living with Tiana helped restore his will to live. As his gloom lifted, he picked up his pen. His newspaper articles called attention to the white man's abuse of the Native Americans.[6]

In 1831 Sam was called home to bury his mother. After the funeral, he met with President Jackson. Jackson asked Sam to keep him informed on affairs in Texas. At that time, Texas belonged to Mexico. The papers Jackson signed made Sam his representative. With them, Sam could move freely through Mexican territory.

Back in Arkansas, Sam sold the trading post. He gave Tiana his house and land. Then he said goodbye and rode south. As far as Sam was concerned, the marriage was over. Late in 1832, he crossed the Red River into Texas.

6

THE STRUGGLE FOR INDEPENDENCE

ᕱᕱᕱᕱᕱᕱᕱᕱᕱ

Texas was all that Sam had dreamed it would be. He wrote to a cousin, "Texas is the finest portion of the globe that has ever blessed my vision."[1]

In San Felipe, Sam hooked up with knife-fighter Jim Bowie. On a trip to San Antonio, the two men talked peace with the Comanches. Back in San Felipe, Sam called on Stephen F. Austin. The founder of Texas must have liked the newcomer. Sam left the meeting with the rights to a league of land—4,428.4 acres. Austin's price was $375 (8¢ an acre). Sam paid for the land with "a fine American horse."[2]

Early in 1833, Sam opened a law office in Nacogdoches. By Mexican law, lawyers had to be Catholic. That was fine with Sam. As required, he took a saint's name. Then he talked a priest into baptizing him.[3] At night Samuel Paul Houston took Spanish lessons from Anna Raguet. He fell in love, but Anna kept him at arm's length.

For Texans, life under Mexican rule was becoming harder to bear. In June 1832, blood was shed in a clash between settlers and army troops. To avoid further conflict, a convention met in April 1833 at San Felipe. Sam's neighbors sent him to speak for them. At that time, Texas was part of the state of Coahuila. The delegates voted to ask Mexico to make Texas a state in its own right. Austin carried the request to Mexico City. President Antonio López de Santa Anna, newly risen to power, turned him down.

Sam's old shoulder wound still pained him. Soaking in the mineral baths at Hot Springs, Arkansas, restored his health. When he returned, angry Texans were cursing Santa Anna. Sam counseled patience. If war broke out, he said, Mexico would win. The Texas militias would be no match for a modern army.

In 1835 a Mexican officer jailed two Texas traders. The act started a new round of trouble. Led by William Travis, a makeshift force of Texans freed the traders. Santa Anna sent General Martín Cós to tame the settlers. Austin called on Texans to prepare to fight. In Nacogdoches, Sam took command of the town militia. "The morning of glory is dawning upon us," he told his men. "The work of Liberty has begun."[4]

At Gonzales, settlers guarded a small brass cannon. When a Mexican force came to seize the gun, the Texans stood firm. A volley of rifle fire forced the troops to retreat. A bigger triumph followed at San Antonio. After a short siege, General Cós surrendered the city. The easy triumphs did not fool Sam. The Texans had been facing troops who were poorly led and badly equipped. Battle-tested regulars would soon take over the fighting.

A new convention met at San Felipe. Still trying to avoid a fight, its leaders again asked for statehood. Santa Anna's answer was to lead his army northward. Faced with

Sam Houston never saw much of what is now the state of Texas. When he died in 1863, settlers had pushed only halfway across the huge state.

this threat, the convention asked Sam to serve as commander-in-chief of the Texas forces. Sam said he needed five thousand men. Because the army relied on volunteers, the goal was never met. When he tried to unite his scattered forces, his orders were ignored.[5]

In January 1836, Sam ordered William Travis to leave the Alamo. Travis refused. He believed the fortress could withstand a siege. In the end, the courage of the Alamo's defenders was not enough. All of the Texans died in Santa Anna's final assault on March 6. At Goliad, James Fannin also ignored Sam's orders. Trapped there by Mexican troops, he was forced to give up. Santa Anna's men shot Fannin and four hundred prisoners on March 27.

Sam had turned forty-three on March 2, the same day Texas declared its independence. Now it was up to Sam and his men to finish the job. In the weeks that followed, he pulled back as Santa Anna advanced. His soldiers grumbled and complained. Some quit the army. At last, on April 21, Sam found a field to his liking. In the smoke and flames of San Jacinto, the Republic of Texas won its freedom.

7

FROM INDEPENDENCE TO STATEHOOD

〜〜〜〜〜〜〜〜〜〜

The war left the hero of San Jacinto with two major problems. The first involved his purse. Texas could not pay Sam for his war service. The second involved his health. His wounded leg was badly inflamed.

In mid-May, Sam sailed to New Orleans for treatment. A crowd cheered as he limped off the boat. A moment later he collapsed on the dock. Friends rushed him to a doctor, who cut out bone chips and rotted flesh. Sam limped on that leg until the day he died.

That fall, Texas picked its first president. Stephen F. Austin and Henry Smith ran for the office. The people did not want either man. They wanted Sam Houston. Eleven days before the election, Sam bowed to the pressure. His fellow Texans gave him 80 percent of their votes.[1]

Sam was sworn in on October 22, 1836. His government met in Columbia, the new capital. President Houston lived in a hut with dirt floors. He stuffed rags into the windows because there was no glass. Sam and Secretary of State Austin wanted Texas to join the Union. The United States balked. Some Americans argued that making Texas a state would lead to war with Mexico. Abolitionists screamed even louder. They hated the thought of adding a new slave state to the Union.

In 1837, Sam divorced Eliza. Tiana had died of a fever. Single once more, he renewed his pursuit of Anna Raguet. Anna enjoyed his courtship, but would not say yes to his marriage proposal. A failed romance, however, was the least of Sam's problems. Texas was a million dollars in debt. Native American raids were on the rise. Sam had to use his own funds to help feed the army. Half of his navy was stranded in New York harbor. Texas could not pay the shipbuilding costs.

Lured by cheap rents, Sam moved the capital to Houston. The new town had been named in his honor. To cut costs, he

Sam Houston took office as the President of Texas in October 1836. His capital city, Columbia, was a village. The future of Texas was by no means secure. His new country had less than 60,000 citizens. Houston knew there was a real threat of a second war with Mexico.

reduced the army by two-thirds. His agents in the United States tried to sell Texas bonds, but investors were hard to find. One of Sam's pet projects did work out well. The Texas Rangers brought a measure of law and order to the frontier.

By law, Sam could not succeed himself. In the election of 1838, Mirabeau Lamar won the office. Sam detested Lamar. He took his revenge on the day Lamar was sworn in. Dressed as George Washington, Sam gave a three-hour farewell speech. The sight of Sam in his powdered wig, combined with the length of his address, left Lamar speechless.[2]

Free from his duties, Sam went on tour to talk up the wonders of Texas. In Alabama he met the wealthy Nancy Lea. Sam almost forgot his sales pitch when he saw the widow's violet-eyed daughter. For Margaret Lea and Sam Houston, it was love at first sight.

Back home, friends elected Sam to the state house of representatives. By this time, the free-spending Lamar had moved the capital to Austin. Sam thought the move was wasteful. He also argued that the town was exposed to Native American attack.[3]

Sam, a battle-scarred forty-seven, married twenty-one-year-old Margaret Lea in May 1840. The newlyweds moved into a home on Galveston Bay. To please his bride, Sam gave up hard liquor. He also went to church more often.

In 1841 Sam won a second term as president. To set an example, he refused to live in the mansion Lamar had built. He also switched the capital back to Houston. The people of Austin fought the move by standing guard over the archives.[4] Hotheads in the legislature gave Sam a bigger headache. Their claims to New Mexico and California touched off a brief war with Mexico. Their southern neighbor would be a threat, Sam preached, until Texas joined the Union.

Margaret gave birth to Sam, Jr., in 1843. The proud father was soon back at work, hatching a new plan. To put pressure on the United States, he sought a treaty with Great Britain. The tactic worked. Washington did not want the British to gain a foothold in the Southwest. Three months after Sam's term ended, Congress voted to annex Texas. President John Tyler signed the bill on March 1, 1845.

Sam and Margaret set out to share the great news with Andrew Jackson. Sadly, Sam's old friend died three hours before they reached Nashville.

In 1840 Sam Houston married Margaret Lea, a sheltered young Alabama woman. Despite her ill health, Margaret gave birth to eight children in the early years of their marriage.

8

SAM RETURNS TO WASHINGTON

Sam turned fifty-three in 1846. Margaret hoped he would retire. To her dismay, the Texas legislature chose him to be one of the state's senators. When Sam left for Washington, Margaret's poor health kept her in Texas.

In March, Sam began his two-year term. There was nothing shy about him. On the Senate floor, he wore a cougar skin waistcoat. On the street, he often threw a Mexican blanket over his shoulder.[1]

Oregon was the chief subject of debate that year. In long, fiery speeches, Sam urged the United States to claim the entire territory. Cautious souls argued that doing so would lead to war with Great Britain. War, Sam shot back, was better than losing honor or empire.[2] In time, cooler heads drew the northern border for the Oregon Territory at the forty-ninth parallel.

When war did break out in 1846, it was with Mexico.

Sam was not surprised. Mexico and Texas, he told the Senate, had long been at war.

Margaret, lonely and often ill, missed her husband. Sam loved her, but politics was in his blood. He worked hard to win a full six-year term. His resistance to the spread of slavery hurt his campaign. Southerners called him a traitor. A slave owner himself, Sam promised he would not vote to ban slavery.

The Mexican War ended in February 1848. The peace treaty added half a million square miles to the United States. Would the western lands be free or slave? Sam still believed in the Missouri Compromise of 1820. That law had confined slavery to states below latitude 36°30'. The South cursed Sam anew when he backed the Compromise of 1850. The bill allowed the admission of California as a free state. Texans also complained about losing their claim to New Mexico. Sam told them the state gained more than it lost. One section of the bill canceled the state's old debts.

Sam often came home to find Margaret nursing a new baby. In all, the couple had eight children. After moving to Independence, Sam delighted Margaret by asking to be baptized. Despite his earlier baptism, he had never worshipped as a Catholic. That Sunday churchgoers were shocked to find that local kids had filled the baptismal font with mud. The prank did not let Sam off the hook. The Baptist preacher dunked his convert in the icy waters of nearby Rocky Creek.[3]

In 1852 the Democrats thought of running Sam for

president of the United States. Sam liked the idea. He was already a hero in the North. Now he tried to mend fences in the South. The right to own slaves, he said, could not be taken away. As the clear favorite, Sam thought he had earned the nomination. Party leaders did not agree. They picked Franklin Pierce.

Texas elected Sam to a third Senate term in 1853. A year later, Congress passed the Kansas-Nebraska Act. New states north of 36°30' now could choose to be free or slave. The South saw the act as a chance to add new slave states. Sam feared it would rip the nation apart. As much as he loved the South, he loved the Union more.

In the 1850s, Sam and Margaret Houston lived in this house in Independence, Texas. Sam, Jr., went to Baylor University there. Margaret called Independence the loveliest spot on earth.

Would Kansas be slave or free? In 1856 armed bands fought for the right to make the choice. As blood flowed on the prairie, two new parties were born. The Republicans campaigned to end slavery. Sam was alarmed. Sending a Republican to the White House might force the South to secede.

The newly-formed American party was pro-Union but not antislave. Sam felt at home with the secretive party. Many people called its members the Know-Nothings. Their hatred of immigrants and Catholics did not upset him. For a time, it looked as though Sam would be the Know-Nothing candidate. In the end, the party picked former president Millard Fillmore.

Texans called Sam a traitor and worse. In 1857, two years before his term ended, the legislature picked his successor. Sam stormed back to Texas and entered the race for governor. He blasted his foes, calling them "swindlers," "forgers," and "cowards." Nothing helped. For the first time, the voters turned their backs on Sam.

9

THE FINAL BATTLES

Sam came home in March 1859 after finishing his term in the Senate. All he hoped for, he wrote, was to be with his wife and children. He said he would raise sheep and cattle on his Cedar Point farm.[1] Margaret noted that his limp was worse.

The quiet life ended all too soon. The sight of an old foe running for governor was too much. Sam jumped into the race. Short of funds, he ran without party backing. He made only one speech. In Texas, that was enough. His name was still magic.

The Houstons arrived in Austin in December. The governor's mansion, they found, had been stripped of furniture. The state had to spend $1,500 to make the place livable. Even then, the family was crowded into four upstairs bedrooms. A seven-foot, four-poster bed gave the governor room to stretch out.

Sam spoke out against secession. Texas, he said, "entered not into the North, nor into the South, but into the Union."[2] To fight the drift toward civil war, he proposed a better use of the nation's strength. The United States, Sam declared, should annex Mexico. Doing so, he said, would "improve our neighborhood."[3] Better still, the North-South conflict would end as slavery spread southward. Border raids by Mexican bandits gave added force to Sam's argument. The nation, its mind fixed on the slavery issue, ignored his plan.[4]

The desire to be president still drove Sam. As the election year of 1860 dawned, "Houston men" rallied to his cause. Their support pleased Sam, but it was not enough. The parties met, debated, and picked other men. Calling himself the "people's candidate," Sam stayed in the race. He spoke out for Southern rights—but only within the Union. Electing Lincoln, he thundered, would lead to civil war. It was not long before Sam

As the Civil War drew near, Governor Sam Houston tried to keep Texas from joining the Confederacy. When the state's voters approved secession, Sam refused to take a loyalty oath to the Confederate States. The Texas legislature responded by removing him from office.

Texas has not forgotten Sam Houston. At San Jacinto, a monument of native Texas limestone rises over the coastal plain. Nearby, the San Jacinto Museum of History retells the heroic story of Sam Houston and the winning of Texas independence.

～～～～～～～━ ◆ ━～～～～～～～

saw that he was hurting his own cause. Rather than split the anti-Lincoln vote, he withdrew from the race.

Lincoln won the election. As Sam had forecast, South Carolina left the Union. More slave states followed. The rebels formed the Confederate States of America. Would Texas follow the same path? In February 1861, delegates met in Austin. They declared that Texas was part of the Confederacy. Sam opposed the move, but he had few allies. Given a chance to vote on the issue, Texans favored secession three-to-one. On March 15, state officials were ordered to swear loyalty to the Confederacy.

Sam did not sleep that night. In the morning he said, "Margaret, I will never do it."[5] He was as good as his word. While his fellow officials took the oath, Sam slipped out of the room. A clerk called his name three times. Sam did not respond. Friends found him in a basement room, whittling. The convention replaced him with a new governor.[6]

Two weeks later the Civil War began. White-haired and stooped, Sam offered to serve with the Rebels. His offer was turned down. Sam, Jr., joined the 2nd Texas Volunteers. He fought bravely until he was wounded at Shiloh. The Bible in his pocket absorbed much of the bullet's impact. It very likely saved his life.[7]

By 1863 the Southern cause was failing. Sam's health was no better. In July a cold turned into pneumonia. His breathing grew labored. Family and friends crowded close to say goodbye. On July 26, Sam spoke for the last time. "Margaret! Texas . . . Texas!" he muttered.[8] A moment later the hero of San Jacinto was dead.

That night Margaret opened the family Bible. She wrote, "Died on the 26th of July 1863 Genl Sam Houston, the beloved and affectionate Husband and father, the devoted patriot, the fearless soldier—the meek and lowly Christian."[9] She knew her man. Sam could not have asked for a more fitting epitaph.

NOTES BY CHAPTER

Chapter 1

1. Stephen L. Hardin, *Texian Iliad* (Austin, Tex.: University of Texas Press, 1994), p. 209.

2. Marquis James, *The Raven: A Biography of Sam Houston* (Indianapolis, Ind.: Bobbs-Merrill, 1929), p. 250.

3. David Nevin, *The Texans* (New York: Time-Life, 1975), p. 128.

4. James, p. 252.

5. T. R. Fehrenbach, *Lone Star: A History of Texas and the Texans* (New York: Wings Books, 1968), p. 233.

Chapter 2

1. M. K. Wisehart, *Sam Houston, American Giant* (Washington, D.C.: Robert B. Luce, 1962), p. 7.

2. Marshall De Bruhl, *Sword of San Jacinto: A Life of Sam Houston* (New York: Random House, 1993), p. 21.

3. De Bruhl, p. 26.

4. Marquis James, *The Raven: A Biography of Sam Houston* (Indianapolis, Ind.: Bobbs-Merrill, 1929), p. 19.

5. James, p. 20.

6. Alfred M. Williams, *Sam Houston and the Texas War for Independence* (Boston: Houghton Mifflin, 1893), p. 9.

Chapter 3

1. John Hoyt Williams, *Sam Houston: A Biography of the Father of Texas* (New York: Simon & Schuster, 1993), p. 28.

2. Marshall De Bruhl, *Sword of San Jacinto: A Life of Sam Houston* (New York: Random House, 1993), p. 38.

3. De Bruhl, p. 43.

4. Marquis James, *The Raven: A Biography of Sam Houston* (Indianapolis, Ind.: Bobbs-Merrill, 1929), p. 36.

Chapter 4

1. Donald Day and Harry Ullom, eds., *The Autobiography of Sam Houston* (Norman, Okla.: University of Oklahoma Press, 1954), p. 15.

2. Marshall De Bruhl, *Sword of San Jacinto: A Life of Sam Houston* (New York: Random House, 1993), pp. 58–60.

3. John Hoyt Williams, *Sam Houston: A Biography of the Father of Texas* (New York: Simon & Schuster, 1993), pp. 56–57.

4. De Bruhl, p. 83.

Chapter 5

1. John Hoyt Williams, *Sam Houston: A Biography of the Father of Texas* (New York: Simon & Schuster, 1993), p. 64.

2. David Nevin, *The Texans* (New York: Time-Life, 1975), p. 58.

3. Marshall De Bruhl, *Sword of San Jacinto: A Life of Sam Houston* (New York: Random House, 1993), p. 98.

4. Williams, p. 71.

5. Nevin, p. 58.

6. Marquis James, *The Raven: A Biography of Sam Houston* (Indianapolis, Ind.: Bobbs-Merrill, 1929), pp.148–149.

Chapter 6

1. David Nevin, *The Texans* (New York: Time-Life, 1975), p. 68.

2. Eugene C. Barker, "Houston to Guy M. Bryan, November 15, 1852, SN199," *Texas History Collection* (Austin, Tex.: University of Texas).

3. M. K. Wisehart, *Sam Houston, American Giant* (Washington, D.C.: Robert B. Luce, 1962), p. 114.

4. Nevin, p. 71.

5. T. R. Fehrenbach, *Lone Star: A History of Texas and the Texans* (New York: Wings Books, 1968), p. 201.

Chapter 7

1. John Hoyt Williams, *Sam Houston: A Biography of the Father of Texas* (New York: Simon & Schuster, 1993), p. 168.

2. Jean Fritz, *Make Way for Sam Houston* (New York: Putnam, 1986), p. 54.

3. Marshall De Bruhl, *Sword of San Jacinto: A Life of Sam Houston* (New York: Random House, 1993), p. 269.

4. T. R. Fehrenbach, *Lone Star: A History of Texas and the Texans* (New York: Wings Books, 1968), p. 261.

Chapter 8

1. Jean Fritz, *Make Way for Sam Houston* (New York: Putnam, 1986), p. 66.

2. Sue Flanagan, *Sam Houston's Texas* (Austin, Tex.: University of Texas Press, 1964), p. 85.

3. John Hoyt Williams, *Sam Houston: A Biography of the Father of Texas* (New York: Simon & Schuster, 1993), pp. 293–294.

Chapter 9

1. Jean Fritz, *Make Way for Sam Houston* (New York: Putnam, 1986), p. 66.

2. Marshall De Bruhl, *Sword of San Jacinto: A Life of Sam Houston* (New York: Random House, 1993), p. 382.

3. Sue Flanagan, *Sam Houston's Texas* (Austin, Tex.: University of Texas Press, 1964), p. 159.

4. John Hoyt Williams, *Sam Houston: A Biography of the Father of Texas* (New York: Simon & Schuster, 1993), pp. 316ff.

5. Flanagan, p. 176.

6. Williams, p. 344.

7. De Bruhl, p. 398.

8. Williams, p. 362.

9. De Bruhl, p. 403.

GLOSSARY

abolitionists—People who worked to abolish slavery in the years before the Civil War.

Alamo—A former mission in San Antonio that was fortified by rebellious Texans in February 1836. Texans used the massacre of the defenders as a rallying cry for their independence movement against Mexico.

archives—An organized collection of official government papers.

bar exam—A test that law students must pass before they may become licensed attorneys.

breastworks—A defensive barricade, often chest high and made of logs.

dictator—A ruler who possesses absolute power over a country and its people.

duel—An armed combat between two people fought under strict rules. In the 1800s, duels were often fought to settle a point of honor.

electoral college—Under the U.S. Constitution, the group of people chosen by voters in each state to formally elect the president and vice president of the United States.

ensign—In the U.S. Army of the early 1800s, ensigns were the army's lowest ranking officers.

Fugitive Slave Law—A pre-Civil War law that required the return of runaway slaves to their owners. The law was widely ignored in the nonslave states.

Know-Nothings—A popular name for members of the American party of the mid-1800s. When asked about their entry rites, members were instructed to answer, "I know nothing."

lacrosse—A fast-moving outdoor sport based on a traditional Native American ball game. Attacking players try to score goals by passing a ball with long-handled, webbed sticks.

militia—Part-time soldiers who are called to duty in times of emergency. Today, each state has a militia known as the National Guard.

musket ball—The round iron shot fired by a smoothbore, muzzle-loading musket.

omen—A natural event that is seen as a sign of future good or evil.

Panic of 1837—A national depression that was triggered by bank failures.

plantation—In the era before the Civil War, a large farm worked by slaves. Most plantations in the South grew cotton as their main crop.

secede—To withdraw from a political alliance. The Civil War began after Southern states seceded from the United States in 1860–1861.

siege—An attack on a town or fortress that traps the defenders within their fortified positions.

Spanish moss—A parasitic growth that hangs from the branches of trees in long, matted clusters.

statesman—A political leader who puts service to country above party loyalties.

Texas Rangers—A force of mounted police organized in the 1800s to keep order on the Texas frontier.

MORE GOOD READING ABOUT
SAM HOUSTON

Day, Donald, and Harry Ullom, eds. *The Autobiography of Sam Houston.* Norman, Okla.: University of Oklahoma Press, 1954.

De Bruhl, Marshall. *Sword of San Jacinto: A Life of Sam Houston.* New York: Random House, 1993.

Fehrenbach, T. R. *Lone Star: A History of Texas and the Texans.* New York: Wings Books, 1968. pp. 190–349.

Flanagan, Sue. *Sam Houston's Texas.* Austin, Tex.: University of Texas Press, 1964.

Fritz, Jean. *Make Way for Sam Houston.* New York: Putnam, 1986.

James, Marquis. *The Raven: A Biography of Sam Houston.* Indianapolis, Ind.: Bobbs-Merrill, 1929.

Williams, John Hoyt. *Sam Houston: A Biography of the Father of Texas.* New York: Simon & Schuster, 1993.

Wisehart, M. K. *Sam Houston, American Giant.* Washington, D.C.: Robert B. Luce, 1962.

INDEX